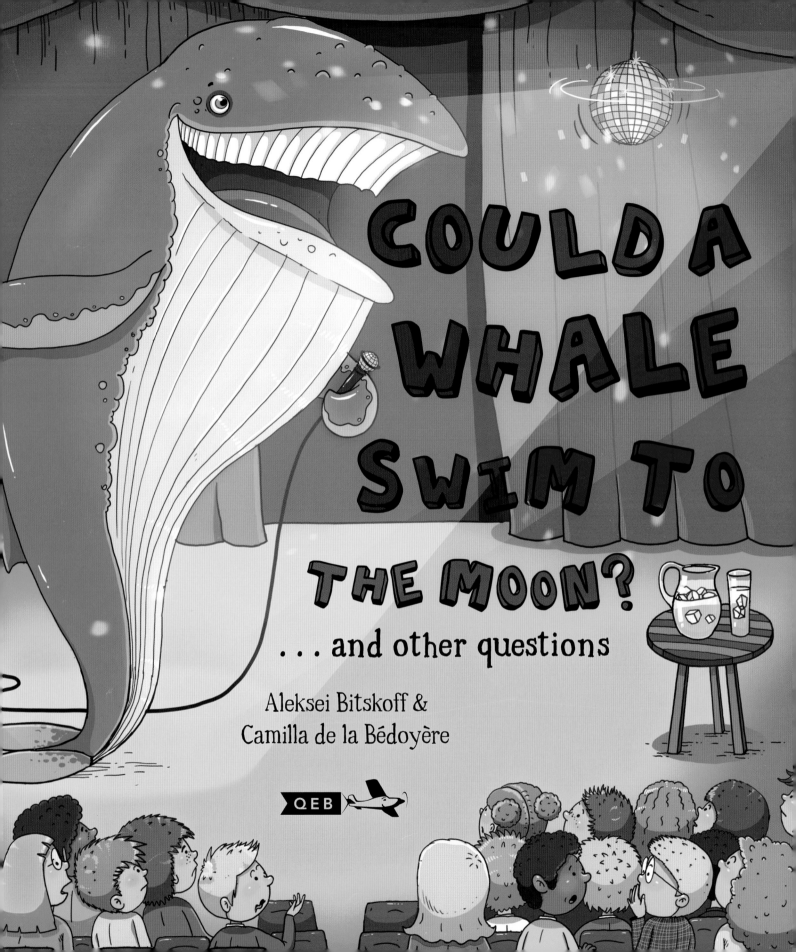

COULD A WHALE SWIM TO THE MOON?

...and other questions

Aleksei Bitskoff &
Camilla de la Bédoyère

QEB

Blue whales are enormous

They look like fish, but whales are mammals, like us.

Design: Duck Egg Blue
Editor: Carly Madden
Editorial Director: Victoria Garrard
Art Director: Laura Roberts-Jensen

First published in the United States by
QEB Publishing, Inc.
3 Wrigley, Suite A
Irvine, CA 92618

www.qed-publishing.co.uk

A CIP record for this book is available from the Library of Congress.

ISBN 978 1 60992 772 1

Printed in China

animals.

Blue whales swim **loooooooong** distances across the ocean.

Imagine if a blue whale came to stay. What would she do?

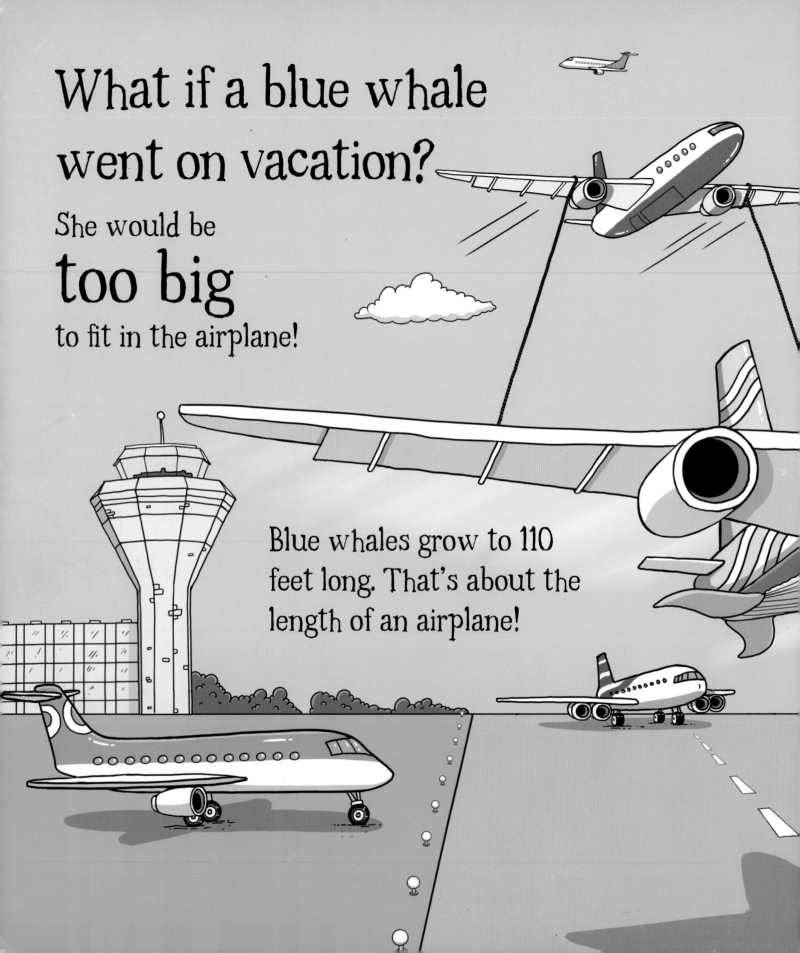

What if a blue whale went on vacation?

She would be
too big
to fit in the airplane!

Blue whales grow to 110 feet long. That's about the length of an airplane!

Blue whales are also very heavy. They weigh about the same as

40 elephants.

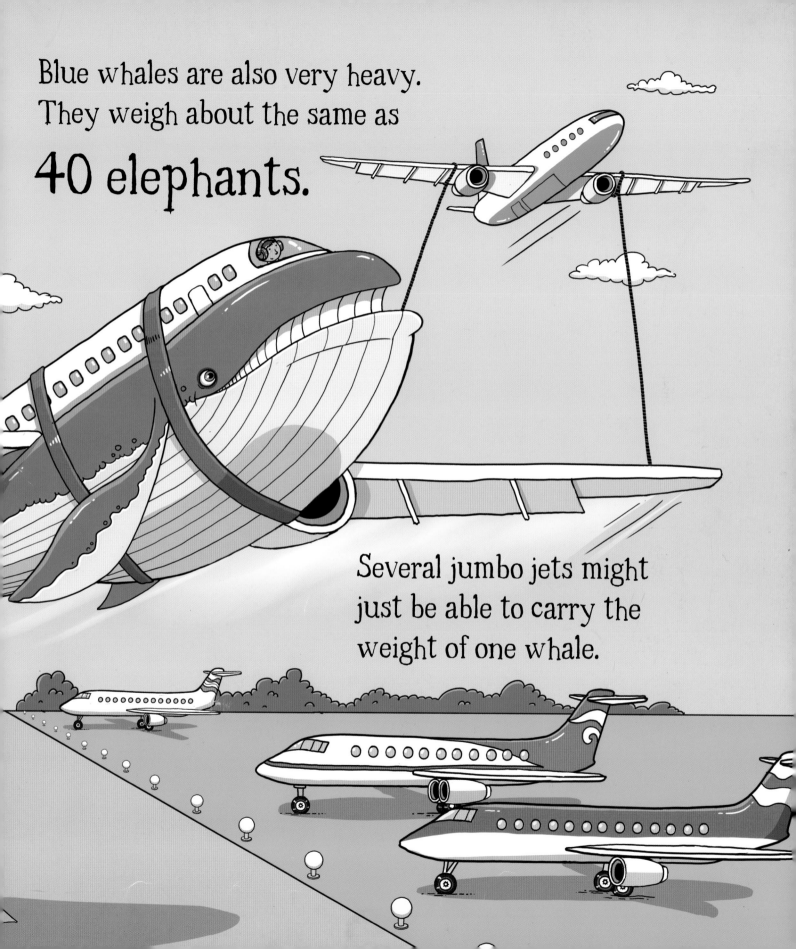

Several jumbo jets might just be able to carry the weight of one whale.

Could a whale swim to the Moon?

During its long life, a blue whale can swim about 620,000 miles.

That's like swimming
around the world

25 times.

It's farther than going to the

Moon and back!

Would a blue whale baby grow as fast as me?

When blue whales are born they weigh 3.3 tons. As a baby they are already one of the **biggest animals** on the planet!

A baby whale can grow
over an inch and put on

200 pounds

in just one day.

That's as much as an
adult man weighs!

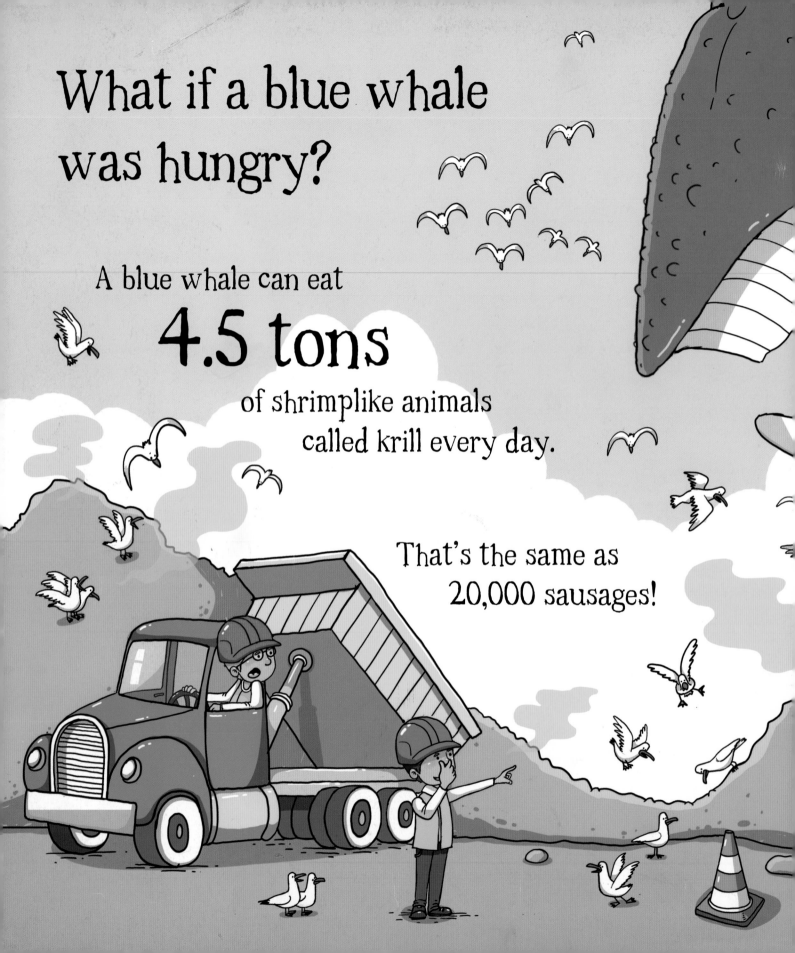

What if a blue whale was hungry?

A blue whale can eat

4.5 tons

of shrimplike animals called krill every day.

That's the same as 20,000 sausages!

Each krill is just
the size of a
jelly bean!

What if a blue whale tried synchronized swimming?

She would be a natural! Blue whales make lots of movements at the water's surface.

They **slap** the water with their fins ... make a splash

Would a whale be a good friend?

She would give ...

... ENORMOUS

What if a whale
threw a party?

She could fill the room with
balloons.

Whales breathe in and out through blowholes in their head. One blue whale breath would be enough to blow up...

250 balloons!

What if a blue whale stayed the night?

She wouldn't need a toothbrush. Her mouth may be massive, but she has

no teeth

at all—not even tiny ones!

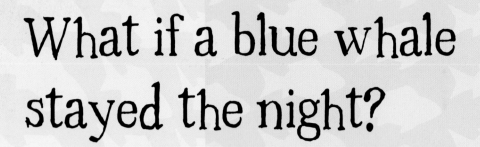

Instead, she has huge combs made of baleen in her mouth. These sieve tiny krill out of the water. Then the whale gobbles them up.

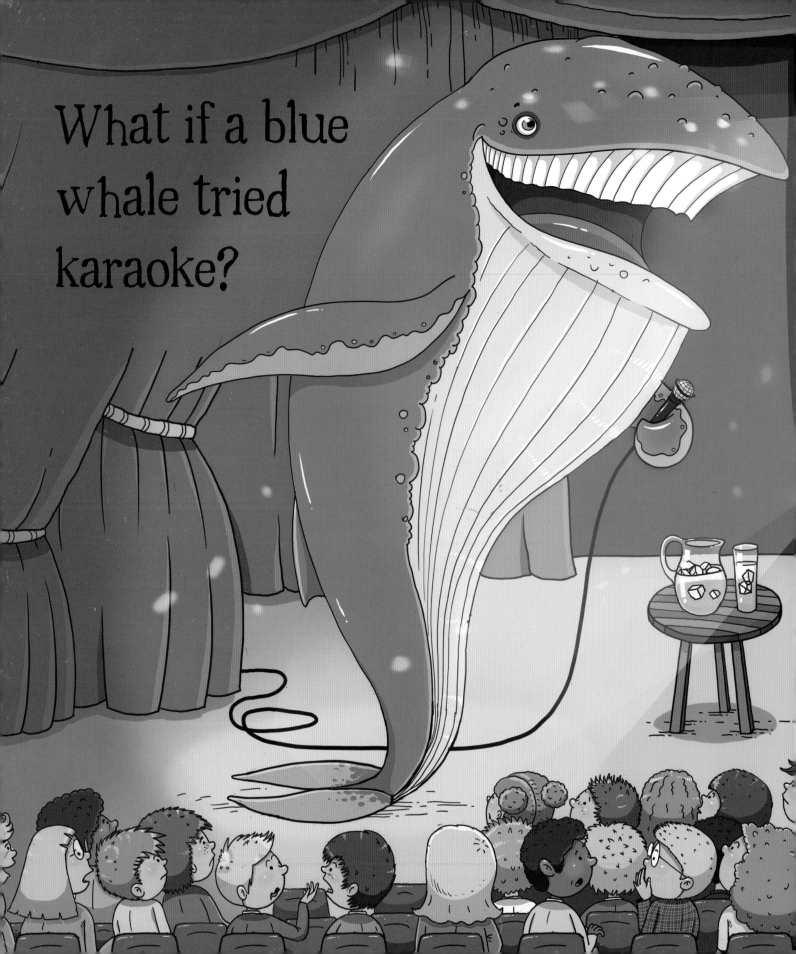

What if a blue whale tried karaoke?

Blue whales **love to sing.**

However, their voices are so deep that we humans **can't hear them!**

Their songs can be heard by other whales far across the ocean. That makes a blue whale the **loudest** animal on the planet.

More about blue whales

Blue whale is pointing to the places where she lives.
Can you see where you live?

FACT FILE

There are 85 types of whale, and the blue whale is the biggest of them all.

Some whales, like the blue whale, only feed on tiny animals, but most of them are hunters that eat seals, fish, and squid.

A blue whale can't swallow anything bigger than a beach ball.

Whales sometimes live together in groups called pods.

A blue whale's tongue is about 13 feet long and weighs as much as an Asian elephant.

Areas where blue whales live

NORTH AMERICA

PACIFIC OCEAN

SOU
AME

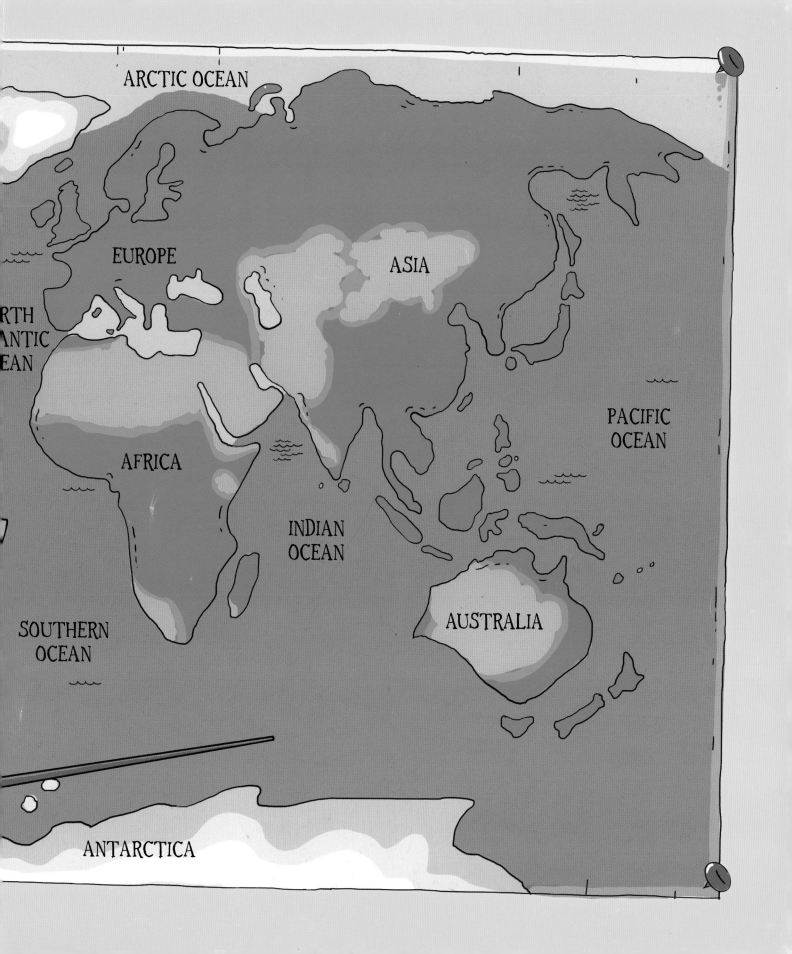

Greetings from the ocean!

POST CARD

It was a great vacation, but I'm glad to be back in the sea. I've been swimming across the ocean, gulping down krill. I can hear my friends calling (they are about 600 miles away, but I've got fantastic hearing!) so I'm going to tell them all about my trip.

Love,
Blue Whale X

SENT BY BLUE WHALE POST
SOUTHERN OCEAN

The Pryce Family
221 Main Street
Boston
02138
USA

5148263560809178379